Welcome to the
Performerati's Cookbook

planet K2

First published in Great Britain in 2018 by PlanetK2

Copyright © PlanetK2 2018

A CIP Catalogue of this book is available from the British Library.

ISBN: 978-0-9927598-5-8

Cover design and typeset by
www.chandlerbookdesign.co.uk

Printed in Great Britain by
4Edge Limited

Welcome to the Performerati's Cookbook

When performance calls, you want to be ready.

Over the years we've been asked to create different ways to help people feel superbly ready to perform and sometimes that means we're working shoulder to shoulder with amazing people, great companies and fabulous brands.

The thing is, we can't always be there to rub shoulders and though we've searched and searched, we can't find our superhero powers so we can be anywhere we're needed. Maybe we left them on a train or threw them out by accident. It's so annoying.

Well, we thought, if you can't get the chefs to come and cook with you and the chefs you need aren't nearly good looking enough to have their own TV series, then a cookbook might work well.

So here it is.

These recipes are for everyday dishes that nourish you and your performance. They're simple, so dive in and give them a right old seeing to. It really doesn't matter if they don't turn out perfect the first time or every time. The more you use the recipe, the more consistent you'll get.

Play with them, add stuff that excites or interests you and let us know how it's going. If you'd like us to put together some new recipes, or to ask us more about the ones in the book, just drop us a line. You can find how to do that on the next page.

This book is to take the mystery out of high performance and make it as sweet as performance pie. Dive in and in no time, you'll be cooking up a storm.

To those who are about to perform, we salute you.

Who are the Performerati?

Some say they can turn darkness into light. Some say they came here to wage endless war against mediocrity. Some say their souls are so restless that they never rest. The truth is out there somewhere and one day, it will be found. Maybe someone left it on a train. Until then, we're just glad they exist.

The Performerati's email address is a secret. Luckily, they've appointed the human performance experts at PlanetK2 to look after their fan mail (we've kept both letters in a safe place) and their email.

You can write to them at theperformerati@planetK2.com

Starters

Appetisers

Sharing platter

Dessert

Starters

High Performer Pie

High Performer Pie

This is the first recipe for a reason. You need to get comfortable with this one before you tackle the others. If you were making a gingerbread house, these would be your gingerbread foundations.

Ingredients:

1 jar of smooth talent is not enough butter

100 grammes of desire to improve flour. Organic is best

3 tablespoons of self-awareness and self-acceptance spice

A decent handful of coachability and humility mix

1 beautifully proportioned performance pie case – you can get these at theperformanceroom.co.uk

1 jug of gently yielding embracing change

High Performer Pie

- Mix the smooth talent is not enough butter with the desire to improve flour. Take your time here until you have a soft but firm mixture with beautifully formed peaks

- Add in the self-awareness and self-acceptance spice, being careful not to damage the seeds

- Thicken it with the handful of coachability and humility mix until it starts to rise all on its own

- Spoon the mix into the performance pie case and pour the embracing change over the top

- Marvel at your firm, flexible and nourishing pie

Zingy Goals Soup

Zingy Goals Soup

This is such a simple and nourishing dish and we think it's one of the best starters ever. Sadly, it's often rushed and made with poor quality ingredients so in recent years, it's popularity has waned. Make it well and it will be your soup of the day, every day. It's a great dish to make with work friends – open a bottle of something good and make it a collective effort.

Ingredients:

Several chunks of playing conditions – think fish finger size

250 ml of helpful attitude stock

1 cube of outcome goal

1 cube of process to get you there

1 cube of belief, attitude and behaviour

A gravy jug of realism

1 stoneground wholemeal feedback loaf

Zingy Goals Soup

- Zap the chunks of playing conditions with the attitude stock

- Blend the 3 cubes of outcome, process and behaviours by hand until the mix is smooth yet stiff

- Pour in the realism

- Break the feedback loaf into nice hefty chunks and dunk them in the soup – it makes this dish a meal on its own

Appetisers

High Performing Team
Rainbow Salad

High Performing Team Rainbow Salad

A bit of advice – only use this dish when you need to be a proper team. If you just need a blend of individual roles, you can skip this one and have a cheese sandwich instead.

Ingredients:

1 family sized pack of shared purpose

Individually wrapped high performing team members (see the high performer pie recipe for making these) for the lattice

A small jug of goal and role clarity glaze to bind the lattice together

1 jar of fresh challenge and support

A generous handful of ready mixed control, confidence and connectedness

3 pods each of learning and feedback

1 high performing team leader

- While it's cooking, regularly baste the entire dish with glugs of feedback and fistfuls of learning

- Finally, blend in a high performance leader to keep the dish nice and tight and firm to the touch

High Performing Leader Nuggets

High Performing Leader Nuggets

Who doesn't love a high performing leader? It's another staple dish and perfect whatever the weather. Seldom served on its own, it goes beautifully with High Performing Teams and really brings out the flavour of the High Performer Pie.

Ingredients:

1 family sized pot of responsibility

1 sachet of fresh humility and confidence paradox

300 ml of good coaching stock

1 bucket of freeze dried self-awareness and flexibility granules

2 tablespoons of essence of result obsession

1 pre-prepared high performer pie

3 fistfuls of listening powder

High Performing Leader Nuggets

- Mix the pot of responsibility and swaz it up with the fresh humility and confidence sachet

- Pour in the good coaching stock and dissolve the self-awareness and flexibility granules as you go

- Stir in the essence of result obsession and pour the whole lot over your high performer pie

- Sprinkle the listening powder liberally – don't worry if you get some on yourself, it won't do you any harm

Sharing Platter

Meeting Meze

Meeting Meze

When this dish is properly prepared then everyone can tuck in and have a great time. Too often, some of the ingredients are just tossed in any old how or left out completely. Then your meze is just meh.

Ingredients:

1 family sized pack of shared purpose

Individually wrapped high performing team members (see the high performer pie recipe for making these) for the lattice

A small jug of goal and role clarity glaze to bind the lattice together

1 jar of fresh challenge and support

A generous handful of ready mixed control, confidence and connectedness

3 pods each of learning and feedback

1 high performing team leader

Meeting Meze

- Dial the meeting room temperature to be just right - be ready for this to be wrong for at least half the people at the meeting

- Roll out a solid base of outcome clarity. Spend time getting this right otherwise the whole dish will fall apart

- Blend a fistful of role clarity for everyone there

- Get everyone to toss in the relevant experience and expertise they've brought along

- Keep an eye on your outcome clarity base during the meeting otherwise you risk it getting soggy

- Continue to add good quality fuel and lots of water

Dessert

Performance Review Pavlova

Performance Review Pavlova

What better way to finish the meal than with a delicious Performance Review Pavlova? Simple to put together and wonderfully sweet and rich.

Ingredients:

Egg whites, laid only by free roaming hens who are obsessed with performance or results

100 ml of curiosity & candidness vinegar

2 tablespoons of celebrate success sugar

2 tablespoons of commitment to dissatisfaction essence

1 palm sized portion of disregard for hierarchy

1 bucketload of psychological safety

1 medium punnet of searching question berries

Performance Review Pavlova

- Whisk the egg whites until they are smooth and glossy. For every egg white laid by a result obsessed hen, add 4 laid by their performance obsessed sisters

- Whisk in the vinegar, sugar and essence

- Fold the disregard for hierarchy with the psychological safety and spread that out so that it forms a solid base with nice solid sides

- Spoon everything you've whisked into the middle, spreading it out within the base

- Bake for as long as it takes and carefully place the searching question berries on the top so that everyone gets to eat a range of deliciously sweet searching questions

You Will. Be Ready.

The Performerati hope you've had fun with these recipes.

If you're serious about performance & want to
know more, head over to:

planetK2.com

theperformanceroom.co.uk

planet K²